World's Weirdest Plants

African Acacia Trees Protect Themselves!

By Janey Levy

Gareth Stevens
PUBLISHING

Please visit our website, www.garethstevens.com. For a free color catalog of all our high-quality books, call toll free 1-800-542-2595 or fax 1-877-542-2596.

Library of Congress Cataloging-in-Publication Data

Names: Levy, Janey, author.
Title: African acacia trees protect themselves! / Janey Levy.
Description: New York : Gareth Stevens Publishing, [2020] | Series: World's weirdest plants | Includes index. | Summary: "Many trees provide food for animals. However, some trees-such as the African acacia, or thorn, tree-object to being eaten. And they've developed several clever ways to protect themselves, including thorns, chemical defenses, and ant guards. "– Provided by publisher.
Identifiers: LCCN 2019026843 | ISBN 9781538246276 | ISBN 9781538246283 (library binding) | ISBN 9781538246269 (paperback) | ISBN 9781538246290 (ebook)
Subjects: LCSH: Acacia–Juvenile literature.
Classification: LCC QK495.M545 L48 2020 | DDC 583/.633–dc23
LC record available at https://lccn.loc.gov/2019026843

First Edition

Published in 2020 by
Gareth Stevens Publishing
111 East 14th Street, Suite 349
New York, NY 10003

Copyright © 2020 Gareth Stevens Publishing

Designer: Katelyn E. Reynolds
Editor: Abby Badach Doyle

Photo credits: Cover, p. 1 Nick Garbutt/Nature Picture Library/Getty Images; cover, pp. 1–24 (background) Conny Sjostrom/Shutterstock.com; cover, pp. 1–24 (sign elements) A Sk/Shutterstock.com; p. 5 EcoPrint/Shutterstock.com; p. 7 Andreas 06/Wikipedia.org; p. 9 (center acacia tree) ararat.art/Shutterstock.com; p. 9 (leaves, flowers, pods) Bettina Calder/Shuttestock.com; p. 9 (thorns) DaweArt/Shutterstock.com; p. 11 Giampaolo Cianella/Shutterstock.com; p. 13 MicheleB/Shutterstock.com; p. 15 (main) cpaulfell/Shutterstock.com; p. 15 (inset) Carol Farneti-Foster/Oxford Scientific/Getty Images; p. 17 (main) Johan Elzenga/The Image Bank/Getty Images; p. 17 (inset) Mary Ann McDonald/Corbis Documentary/Getty Images; p. 19 Daryl & Sharna Balfour/Gamma-Rapho via Getty Images; p. 21 (main) Joe Sohm/Visions of America/Universal Images Group via Getty Images; p. 21 (inset) SEYLLOU DIALLO/AFP/Getty Images.

All rights reserved. No part of this book may be reproduced in any form without permission in writing from the publisher, except by a reviewer.

Printed in the United States of America

Some of the images in this book illustrate individuals who are models. The depictions do not imply actual situations or events.

CPSIA compliance information: Batch #CW20GS : For further information contact Gareth Stevens, New York, New York at 1-800-542-2595.

CONTENTS

Words in the glossary appear in **bold** type the first time they are used in the text.

ALL ABOUT AFRICAN ACACIA TREES

Trees are wonderful plants. They provide shade on hot summer days. They give us food, such as fruit and nuts. Their leaves supply food for animals, too. But some trees—such as African acacia (uh-KAY-shuh) trees—don't like having their leaves eaten. So, they use strange and clever ways to **protect** themselves.

African acacia trees are some of Africa's best-known trees. Pictures of them commonly appear on the covers of books about Africa. In this book, you'll discover more about these weird plants!

SEEDS OF KNOWLEDGE

There are more than 100 different kinds of acacia trees around the world. While they are all a little different, they share many features.

African acacia trees are also called thorn trees or umbrella trees.

WHERE DO THEY GROW?

You may already know that Africa is a huge **continent**. So where exactly in this giant place are acacia trees found? They're found in eastern and southern Africa. In eastern Africa, they grow on the savanna. This is grassland with scattered trees. It's a hard place to grow because it's dry for half the year. But acacias do well here.

In southern Africa, acacia trees are found on the veld. That's the name given to open farmland in this part of Africa.

SEEDS OF KNOWLEDGE

Acacia trees are only found in warm places. This includes Africa and also parts of Australia, the Americas, and Asia. They need **temperatures** above 64°F (18°C) to grow.

Where to Find African Acacia Trees

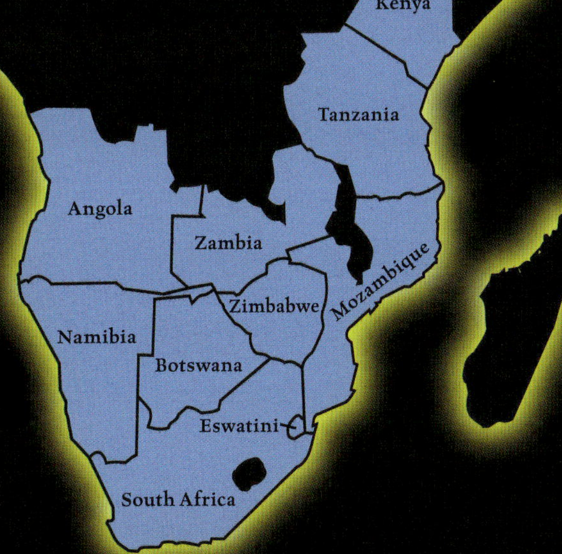

In eastern Africa, acacia trees are found in countries such as Tanzania and Kenya. In southern Africa, they're found in countries such as South Africa, Mozambique, Botswana, Eswatini, Angola, Namibia, Zambia, and Zimbabwe.

UNUSUAL PARTS

How would you recognize an African acacia tree? Well, they often have an umbrella-shaped **canopy**. Many have feathery leaves. But instead of leaves, some have flattened leaf stalks, or stems, called phyllodes (FY-lohdz). These help stop water loss. That's important in the hot, dry places where the trees grow. Thorns hide among the leaves.

In summer, acacias produce round bunches of small yellow or white flowers. **Pollinated** flowers create seedpods. These may fall to the ground unopened or break open before falling.

SEEDS OF KNOWLEDGE

African acacia trees can grow to be quite tall, even though they live where it's hard to grow. They may grow to be as tall as a six-story building—66 feet (20 m) tall!

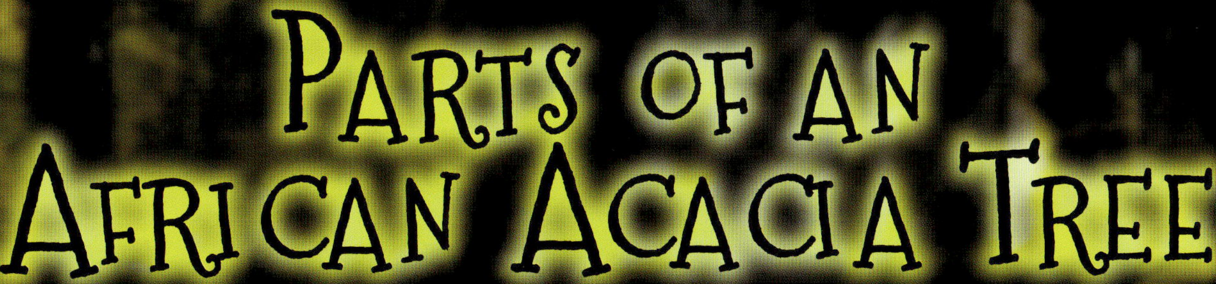

Parts of an African Acacia Tree

leaves

flowers

thorns

pods

Sometimes African acacia trees have straight thorns. Other times, the thorns may have a hook, or curve, on the end.

IT STARTS FROM A SEED

Like many plants you may know, African acacia trees start from seeds. Animals such as giraffes, rhinoceroses, and elephants eat the seedpods. Then, they spread the seeds when they poop!

New trees grow from the seeds. In summer, they produce flowers. The flowers must be pollinated to produce more seedpods. You may be surprised to discover how that happens. Scientists think bugs pollinate many African acacias. That's not unusual. But for at least one kind of African acacia, giraffes do the job!

SEEDS OF KNOWLEDGE

Sometimes seeds may land in conditions that aren't right for growing. Some types of acacia seeds can stay in a resting state for up to 50 years without losing their ability to grow.

This giraffe is enjoying a tasty treat while it pollinates the tree's flowers.

TRICKY THORNS

Many animals—such as giraffes, elephants, and **antelopes**—like to dine on the leaves of African acacia trees. So the trees have come up with ways to protect themselves from these herbivores (UHR-buh-vohrz), or plant-eating animals.

One way the trees protect themselves is with thorns spread along the branches. The thorns are quite sharp, so biting on one would hurt. Herbivores still feed on the trees, but the thorns help keep them from eating too many leaves.

SEEDS OF KNOWLEDGE

It might surprise you to learn the thorns aren't a big problem for giraffes. That's because the giraffe's special tongue can wrap around the branches to avoid the thorns as it reaches for leaves.

Since antelopes aren't as tall as giraffes and elephants, they often stand up on their back legs to eat the leaves of acacia trees.

AN ARMY OF ANTS

Did you know some kinds of African acacia trees have a whole army to protect them? That army is made up of ants!

The acacia trees produce nectar to draw the ants to them. The ants come and makes nests in the trees to be near the nectar. They become guards of the trees to protect their homes and the nectar they eat. When herbivores come along to eat the tree's leaves, the ants attack them and drive them away.

SEEDS OF KNOWLEDGE

The ants don't just drive away large herbivores—they also drive off leaf-eating bugs. They'll even attack bacteria that could harm the acacia tree!

The acacia trees and the ants both benefit from living closely together. This type of **relationship** is called symbiosis (sihm-bee-OH-suhs).

ants feeding on nectar

WHEN TREES ATTACK!

Acacias aren't content with having two **weapons** to fight off herbivores. They also make **chemicals** to guard themselves! Some acacias produce a toxin, or poison, when their leaves are being eaten. This toxin, called tannin, makes leaves taste bad and causes herbivores to quit eating.

Tannin can kill an herbivore if it eats enough of it. In addition, the trees give off ethylene (EH-thuh-leen) gas, which warns other acacias about the danger. Soon, nearby trees produce tannin in their leaves, too. That's pretty clever!

SEEDS OF KNOWLEDGE

When an acacia tree makes ethylene gas, it can travel up to 50 yards (46 m). When nearby trees **detect** it, they start to produce more leaf tannin within just 10 minutes!

This elephant is enjoying these acacia leaves now. But soon tannin will make the leaves taste too bad to eat, and ethylene gas will warn nearby acacias to make tannin, too.

WHAT HAPPENS IF HERBIVORES DISAPPEAR?

You'd think it would be good for acacias if herbivores weren't there to eat the leaves. But that isn't necessarily true.

Scientists discovered that without herbivores, one kind of acacia quits providing food and homes for the ants that protect it. This allows "bad" ants that don't protect the tree to move in. Those ants depend on beetle larvae to make holes for them to live in. Beetle holes harm the tree and hurt its growth. Maybe a little danger is a good thing!

SEEDS OF KNOWLEDGE

Whistling thorn trees that have "bad" ants and beetle larvae are less healthy. They die twice as often as trees that are regularly eaten by large African herbivores.

The African acacia known as the whistling thorn tree stops supplying sweet nectar and homes for its protective ants if herbivores aren't eating its leaves.

ONE TREE, MANY USES

African acacias have many ways to protect themselves from herbivores. However, people have learned ways around the tree's tricks! People have found many uses for these interesting trees.

People feed the leaves, flowers, and seedpods to their livestock. In some places, people eat the seedpods. The trees' tannin is used to turn animal hides into leather and in dyes and inks. The wood is used for fires, building houses, and making tools. And people have even more uses for these amazing, clever trees!

SEEDS OF KNOWLEDGE

An African acacia tree called the gum acacia makes matter called gum arabic. It's used in paints, candy, dyes, inks, and the making of silk, paper, and makeup.

African acacia trees can be used to make many beautiful and useful things. Some trees are even used to make **medicines**.

gum arabic

GLOSSARY

antelope: an animal much like a deer that lives in Africa and southwest Asia

canopy: the upper branches of a tree or forest

chemical: matter that can be mixed with other matter to cause changes

continent: one of Earth's seven great landmasses

detect: to notice or discover the existence of something

medicine: a drug taken to make a sick person well

pollinate: to take pollen from one flower, plant, or tree to another

protect: to keep safe

relationship: the way in which two or more things are connected

temperature: how hot or cold something is

weapon: something used to fight an enemy

FOR MORE INFORMATION

BOOKS

Alderton, David. *Savannas.* Chicago, IL: World Book, 2014.

Diaz, Joanne Ruelos. *Animals on the African Savanna.* North Mankato, MN: Picture Window Books, 2014.

Gregory, Josh. *African Savanna.* Ann Arbor, MI: Cherry Lake Publishing, 2016.

WEBSITES

Acacia
animals.sandiegozoo.org/plants/acacia
Learn more about acacias and how they're used on this website.

Got My Back? Acacia Trees, Ants Help Each Other
www.sciencebuzz.org/blog/got_my_back_acacia_trees_ants_help_each_other
Discover more about the special friendship between acacia trees and ants on this site.

Tropical Savanna: Plants
www.cotf.edu/ete/modules/msese/earthsysflr/savannahP.html
Find out more about African acacias' adaptations here.

Publisher's note to educators and parents: Our editors have carefully reviewed these websites to ensure that they are suitable for students. Many websites change frequently, however, and we cannot guarantee that a site's future contents will continue to meet our high standards of quality and educational value. Be advised that students should be closely supervised whenever they access the Internet.

INDEX